NEVADA GHOST TOWN TRAILS

By MICKEY BROMAN

Revised Edition

Gem Guides Book Co.
315 Cloverleaf Drive, Suite F
Baldwin Park, CA 91706

Library of Congress Catalog Card Number 72-94635
ISBN 0-935182-09-8

PREFACE

The general concept of what constitutes a ghost town will vary from person to person. There are many towns in Nevada with sizable populations that are just ghosts of their former selves, such as Tonopah, Goldfield, Austin and many other old mining towns. Some people consider these ghost towns, others do not. Most towns like this are not included in this book as they can be easily located on road maps.

Some ghost towns have several buildings standing while others have been razed for tax purposes or destroyed by vandals and the elements. Several of these sites are included for the benefit of relic hunters, treasure hunters and historians.

NEVADA LOCATOR MAP

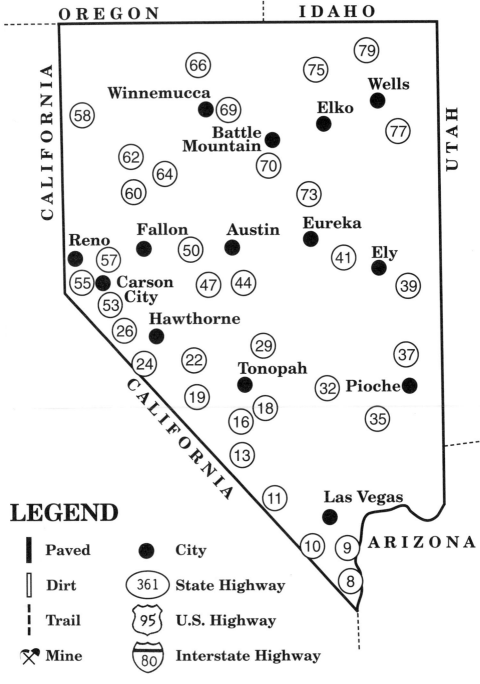

OREGON | IDAHO

CALIFORNIA

UTAH

ARIZONA

79

66 75

Wells

Winnemucca

58 69 Elko

Battle 77
Mountain

62 70

64

60 73

Fallon Austin Eureka

Reno 50 Ely
57 41

55 Carson 47 44 39
53 City

Hawthorne

26

29

24 22 37

Tonopah

19 32 Pioche

16 18 35

13

11 Las Vegas

10 9

8

LEGEND

| Paved
▮ Dirt
⋮ Trail
⚒ Mine

● City
(361) State Highway
(95) U.S. Highway
(80) Interstate Highway

* NUMBER IN CIRCLE INDICATES
THE PAGE ON WHICH THE AREA
MAP MAY BE FOUND

ILLUSTRATIONS

Cover Photo:
Rhyolite

GHOST TOWN INDEX

GHOST TOWN INDEX

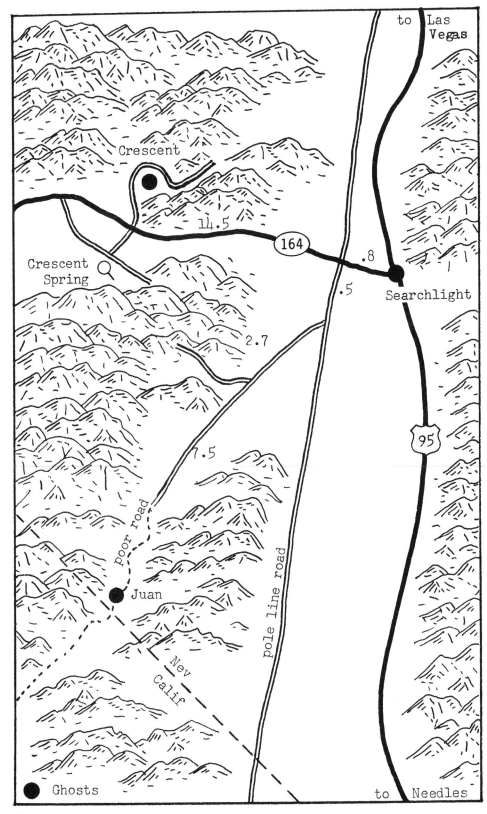

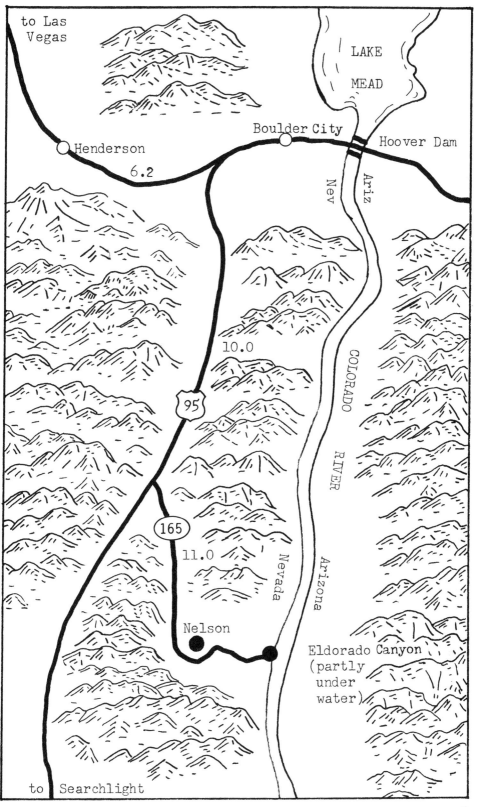

to Las
Vegas

LAKE

MEAD

Henderson

6.2

Boulder City

Hoover Dam

Nev

Ariz

COLORADO

RIVER

10.0

95

165

11.0

Nevada

Arizona

Nelson

Eldorado Canyon
(partly
under
water)

to Searchlight

9

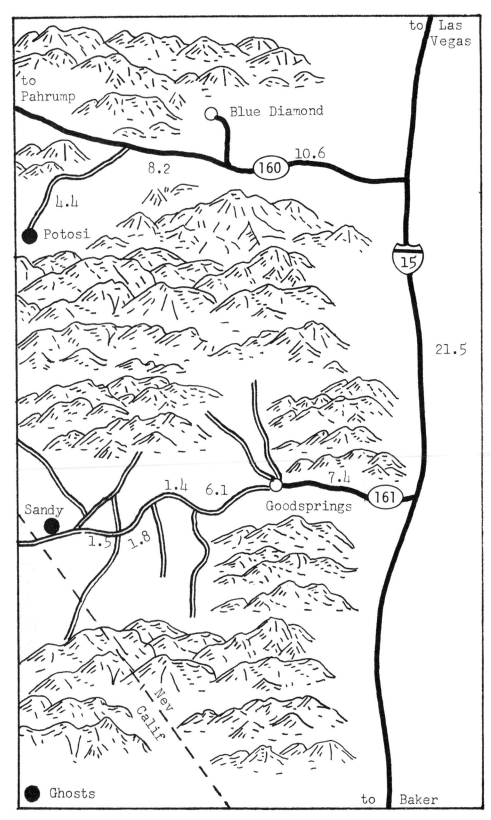

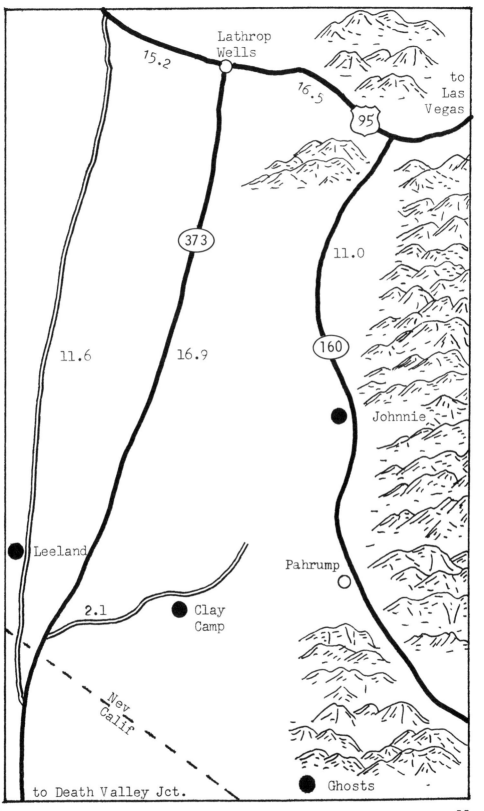

Lathrop
Wells

15.2

16.5

to
Las
Vegas

95

373

11.0

160

11.6

16.9

Johnnie

Leeland

Pahrump

2.1

Clay
Camp

Nev
Calif

to Death Valley Jct.

Ghosts

11

JOHNNIE - The Johnnie and Congress Mines were located
in 1890. The Congress closed down in 1895 and the Johnnie
continued operations until 1913. The camp had a small re-
vival in 1921 when placer gold was discovered. Very little
remains of the town today.

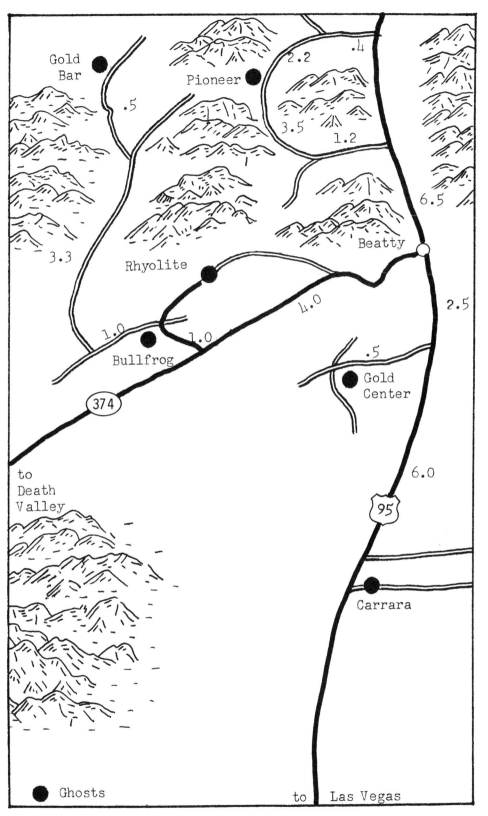

13

CARRARA - The American Carrara Marble Co. started quarrying marble in the Bare Mountains in 1905. A town was platted and named Carrara for the company that supported it. In 1936 it was decided that the marble was too fractured and the quarrying stopped. All that remains today are a few building walls and many stone foundations.

14

RHYOLITE - Gold and silver discoveries were made in the
Bullfrog Hills about 1904 and Rhyolite was established in
1905. The town boomed to a population of over 10,000 people
and by 1912 was completely deserted.

One man, for lack of building material, gathered up
51,000 liquor bottles in 1905 and used them to build his house.
This bottle house still stands today along with the old train
depot and countless stone walls and foundations.

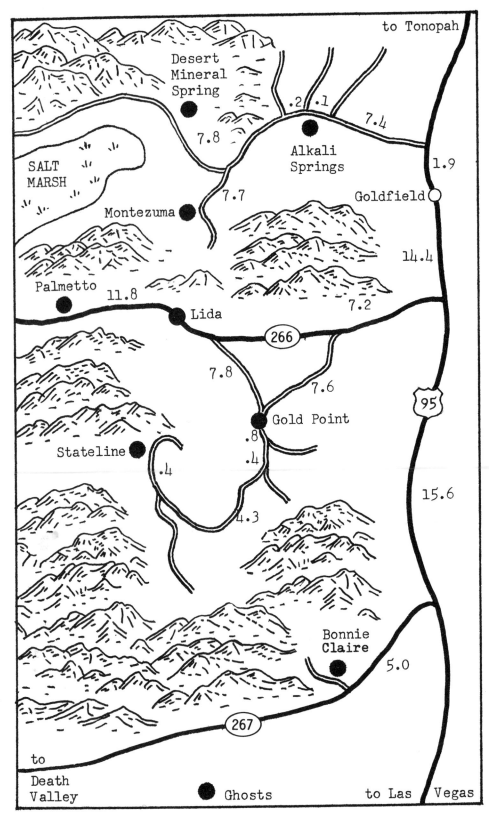

to Tonopah

Desert Mineral Spring

.2 .1

7.4

7.8

Alkali Springs

1.9

SALT MARSH

Goldfield

7.7

Montezuma

14.4

Palmetto

11.8

Lida

7.2

266

7.8

7.6

95

Gold Point

.8

Stateline

.4

.4

.4

4.3

15.6

Bonnie Claire

5.0

267

to Death Valley

Ghosts

to Las Vegas

GOLD POINT - Established about 1908 and originally named Hornsilver, because the principal ore mined here was horn-silver, a silver chloride. The name was changed to Gold Point in 1929 because investors seemed to be more interested in gold than in silver. Peak population reached 2,000 and over $1,000,000 in gold and silver was extracted from the mines. 40 or 50 old buildings are still standing, most of them wooden.

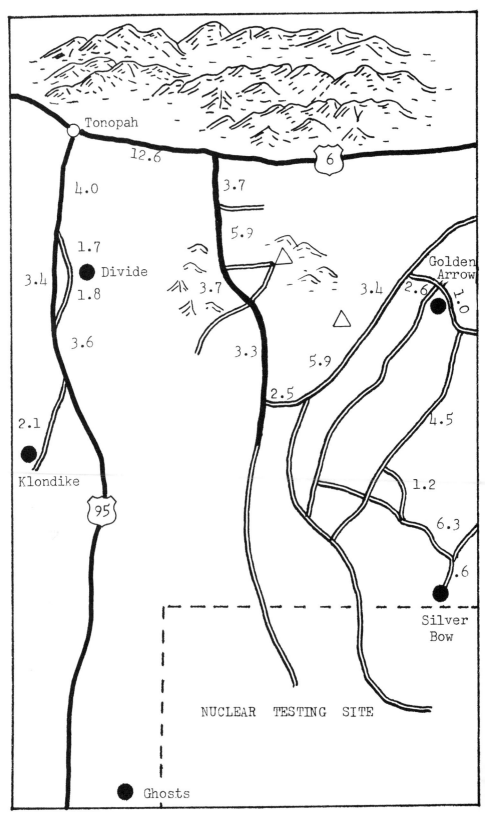

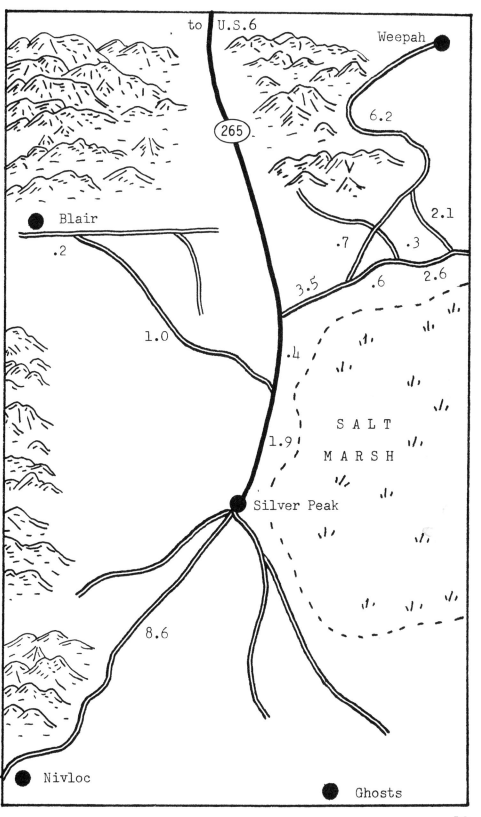

to U.S.6

Weepah

265

6.2

2.1

Blair

.7 .3

.2

3.5 .6 2.6

1.0

.4

S A L T

1.9

M A R S H

Silver Peak

8.6

Nivloc

Ghosts

BLAIR - Blair was a milling town, boasting the largest stamp mill (120 stamps) in Nevada.   The mill was erected in 1907 and shut down in 1915.   The mill foundations and a couple of cement buildings are all that remain today.

Two miles south is the town of Silver Peak which has been a mining town since 1864 and is still thriving today, even though most of the town has been leveled by fires.

WEEPAH - Values were discovered here as late as 1927 and a town sprung up from the desert floor. When word of the discovery got out the rush was on, and dancehall girls from Tonapah were out in their high heeled dancing slippers, staking claims by moonlight. The population s o a r e d to 1,500 and a year later that town was practically deserted.

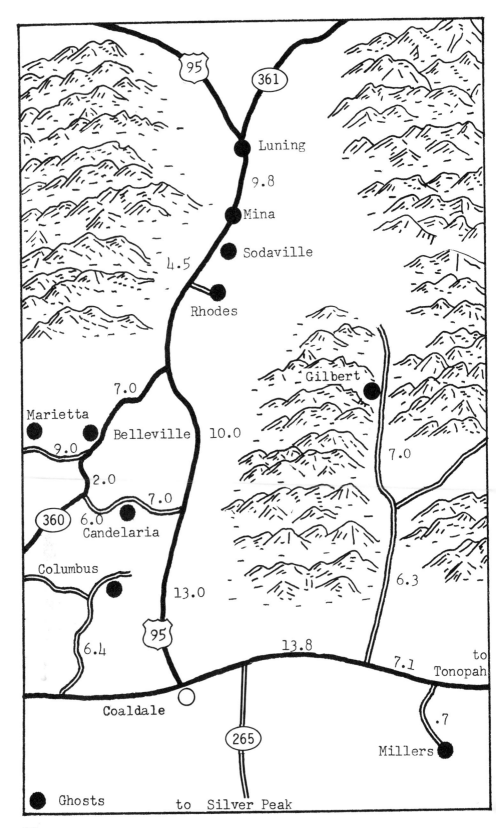

95

361

Luning

9.8

Mina

Sodaville

4.5

Rhodes

Gilbert

7.0

Marietta

Belleville

10.0

9.0

2.0

7.0

7.0

360

6.0

Candelaria

Columbus

13.0

6.3

95

6.4

13.8

7.1

to
Tonopah

Coaldale

.7

265

Millers

Ghosts

to Silver Peak

22

GILBERT - Rich ore discoveries in 1924 brought hordes of prospectors to the area and Gilbert soon had a population of over 500. The town was supported by the Black Mammoth Mine and when the ore vein gave up, so did the town. Only two or three wooden buildings remain today.

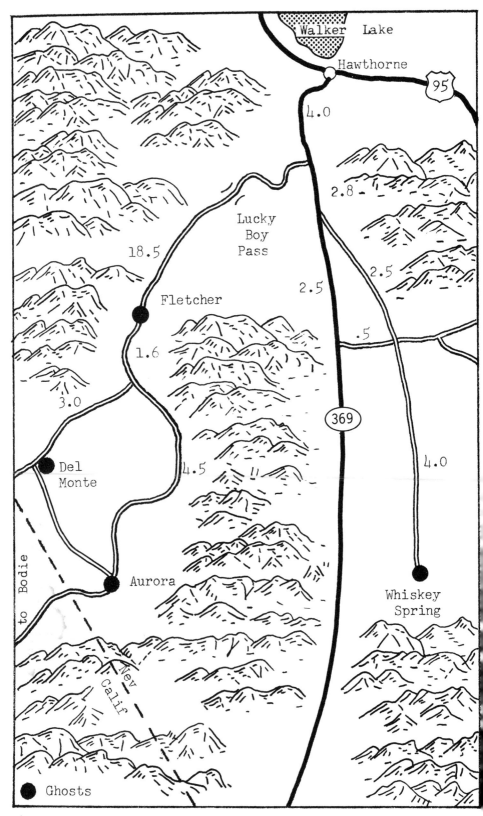

AURORA - Founded in 1860, there was much dispute as to whether Aurora was in Nevada or California, so the town was governed by officials from both states until a survey was made in 1863 and it was determined that the town was 3 miles inside Nevada.

By 1869, $27 million in bullion had been shipped and water was seeping into the mines faster than they could pump it out.

All that remains today is a lot of rubble and extensive ruins of a large, exciting town.

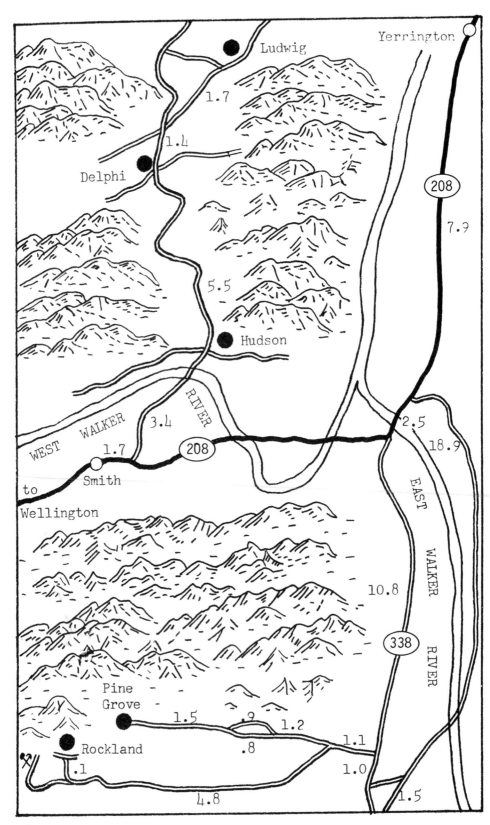

PINE GROVE - Born in 1866 in a pine studded canyon, the town grew to a population of about 300 people. Mining has been done on a large scale here and the mine dumps are huge. Several wooden buildings still stand but they are gradually being destroyed by thoughtless visitors. The canyon abounds with stone ruins and foundations surrounded by pine trees.

ROCKLAND - Gold was discovered in 1868 and the town of Rockland, supported by the Rockland Mine, grew to fair proportions. The mine eventually produced about $1 million before it closed down.

Rockland is situated high on a mountain in a beautiful location in the pines. A few wooden buildings remain, along with the ruins of the old ten stamp mill. This location is difficult to reach in winter months because of snow and unplowed roads.

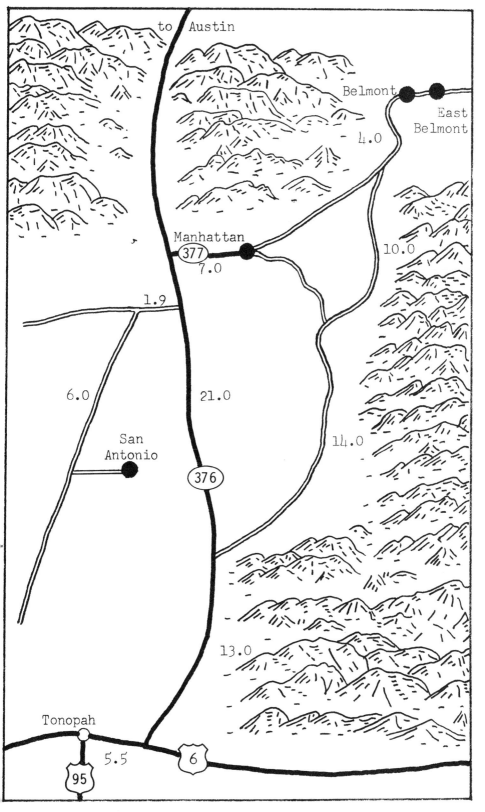

to Austin

Belmont

East
Belmont

4.0

Manhattan
377
7.0

10.0

1.9

6.0

21.0

San
Antonio

376

14.0

13.0

Tonopah

5.5
6

95

BELMONT - Gold and silver values were discovered at the head of Ralston Valley in 1865 and the town of Belmont developed and grew to a peak population of 10,000, to later become the County Seat of Nye County. The mines produced $15 million in gold and silver and 11,000 flasks of mercury before the town finally died in 1903. Some of the ore from the Highbridge Mine assayed over $10,000 per ton but most of it ran about $100 per ton.

The old courthouse and many false front business houses as well as dwellings can still be seen, along with countless foundations and the gaunt frames of the several mills in the area.

EAST BELMONT - Mill ruins just east of Belmont.

31

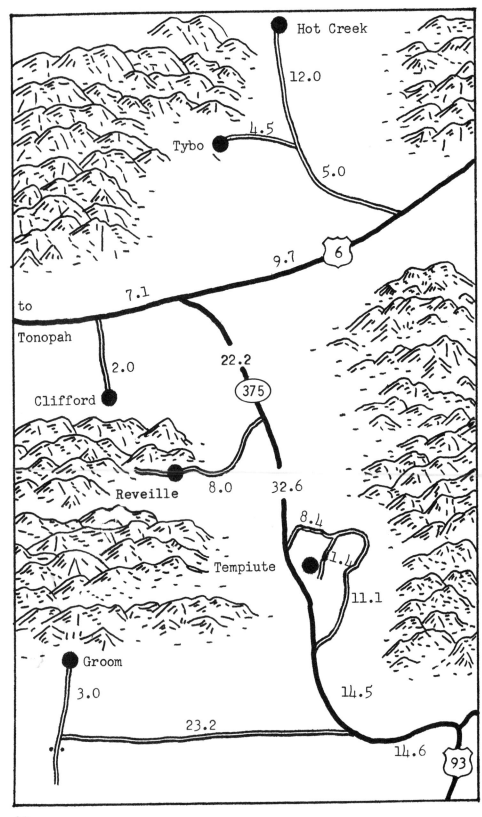

Hot Creek

12.0

Tybo 4.5

5.0

6

9.7

7.1

to

Tonopah

2.0

22.2

375

Clifford

8.0 32.6

Reveille

8.4

1.4

Tempiute

11.1

14.5

Groom

3.0

23.2

14.6

93

32

TYBO - In 1866 an Indian led a prospector to a deposit of ore that assayed $2,000 per ton, and Tybo was born. Tybo was chiefly a producer of silver-lead ores. Occasionally a rich pocket would be uncovered, such as the one at the Slavonian Chief Mine in 1874, which assayed $20,786 to the ton. Nearly $10 million was mined in the area, even though much of the ore was rather low grade ore.

A few buildings and many stone foundations remain today.

REVEILLE - Rich hornsilver deposits were discovered in 1866 and the town of Reveille sprung up. Ore was hauled 140 miles to Austin for three years until a mill was built 12 miles west of town. The mines produced over $4 million in about ten years, and then the vein ran out and Reveille became a ghost. Several rock ruins remain today.

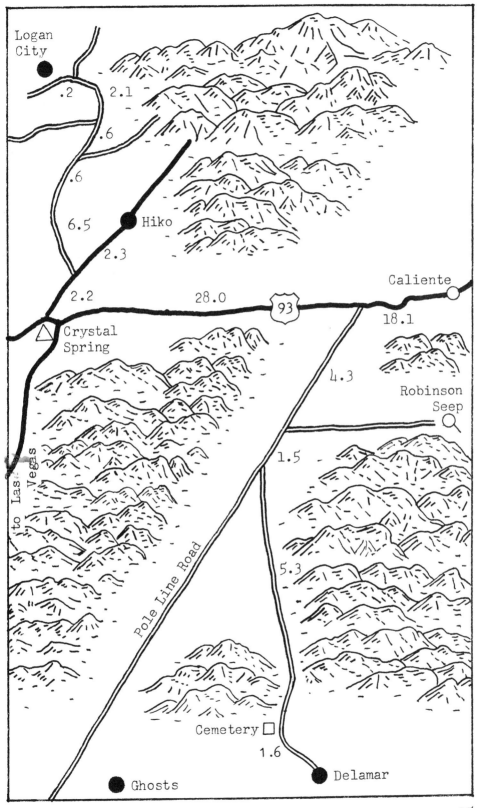

DELAMAR - Men were doomed to die here, and many did, from silicosis caused from breathing the silica dust in the mines. The mines paid high wages ($3.00 per day) to entice husky, healthy farm boys but even the strongest succumbed to the deadly dust. The town grew to immense proportions and the mines produced $25 million in gold and silver from 1892 to 1909 when the town faded and died.

20 or 30 stone buildings still stand, many with the roofs still on and countless foundations extend over a vast area. The grotesque mill tailings are piled high at the edge of town, and when the wind is right a cloud of fine dust can be seen rising from the piles and covering the town like a shroud.

It has been rumored that $70,000 in bullion was hidden here and apparently has never been recovered.

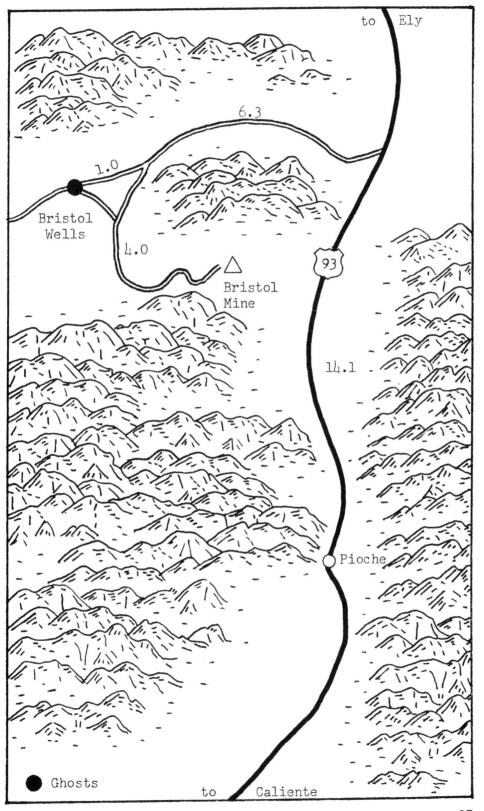

to Ely

6.3

1.0

Bristol
Wells

4.0

△
Bristol
Mine

🛡 93

14.1

◯ Pioche

● Ghosts

to Caliente

37

BRISTOL WELLS - A smelter town of the 1870's. Not much remains of the town today except two stone cabins by a huge black slag pile and three "bee hive" kilns.

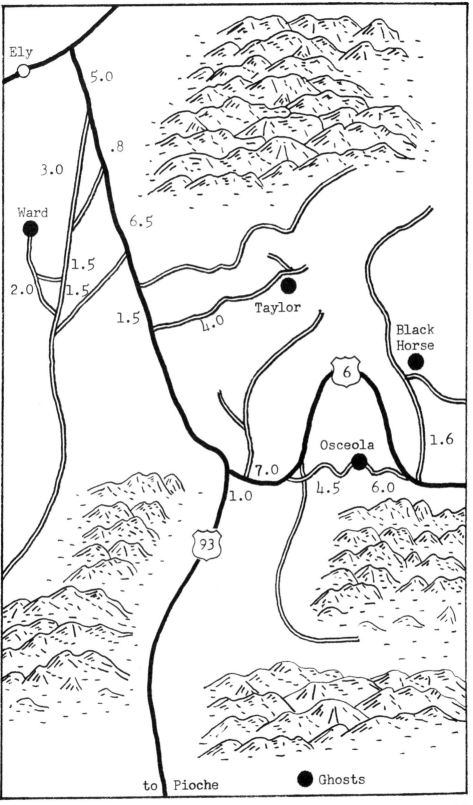

Ely

5.0

.8

3.0

6.5

Ward

1.5

2.0   1.5

1.5

4.0   Taylor

Black
Horse

6

Osceola

1.6

7.0

4.5   6.0

1.0

93

to Pioche   ● Ghosts

OSCEOLA - Established in 1875, Osceola was once a main supply town for ranches all over eastern Nevada. Minerals were discovered and the mines yielded several million dollars in the form of lode and placer gold, silver, lead and tungsten.

Fires have wiped out most of the town. Very few buildings are left to signify the importance of this once busy community.

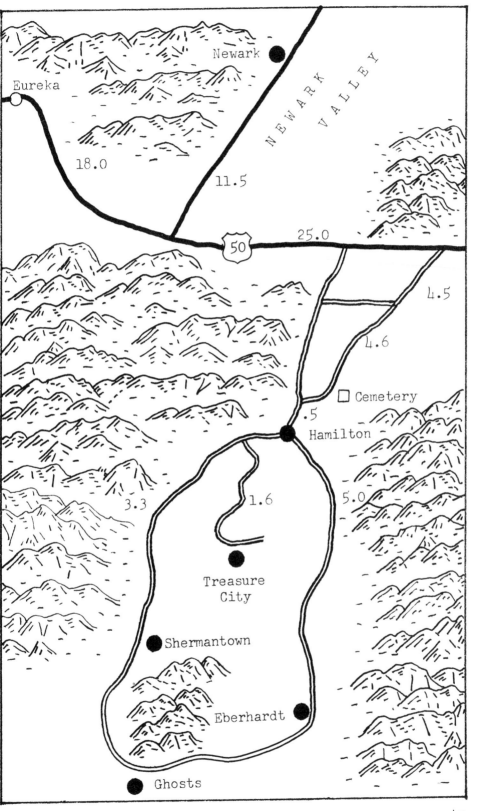

Newark

Eureka

NEWARK VALLEY

18.0

11.5

50 25.0

4.5

4.6

☐ Cemetery

.5

Hamilton

3.3   1.6   5.0

● Treasure
City

● Shermantown

Eberhardt

● Ghosts

41

HAMILTON - The White Pine District was one of the most fabulous silver mining areas in Nevada. Several towns sprung up in the area, supported by 13,000 claims that produced $35 million. The hub of all this activity was Hamilton. The town plat was laid out in 1868 and a year later business lots were selling for $6,000. The population grew to 15,000, but not a soul remains today.

Situated at a 9,000 foot elevation, the town has had a real test of endurance standing up under the heavy snows and icy blasts of hard winters. However, 20 or 30 buildings are still standing, many stone walls and countless foundations. But the tin and building stones are slowly being trucked away by scavengers, and soon a beautiful ghost town will have slipped into oblivion.

TREASURE CITY - Born on a bleak mountain top following rich silver discoveries in 1868 on Treasure Hill. Situated on a blizzard torn peak at an elevation of 10,000 feet, 6,000 people snuggled together trying to keep from freezing through the cold winter months. Water had to be hauled up the mountain, but few people drank it because whiskey was cheaper.

The frame of the old Wells Fargo building still stands and many foundations can be located among the mine dumps on the hill.

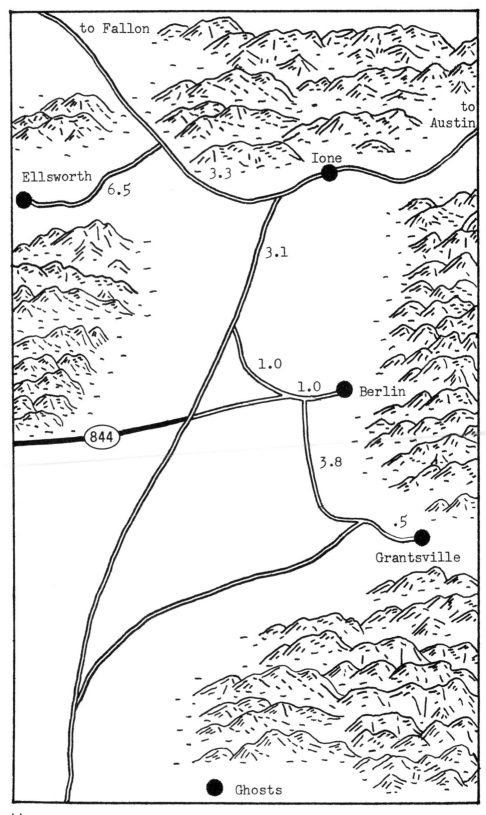

to Fallon

to Austin

Ellsworth 6.5

3.3

Ione

3.1

1.0

1.0 Berlin

844

3.8

.5

Grantsville

Ghosts

BERLIN - A mining town of the late 1800's located at the base of the Shoshone Mountains in the Toiyabe Range. The old boarding house, assay office, and mill buildings are still standing along with a couple of dwellings.

GRANTSVILLE - A small town of the 1870's that reached a peak population of 1,000. Located in a canyon just south of the Ichthyosaur State Park, the town has melted away and only a few buildings are left standing. Many foundations cover the site and the size of the mill tailings that extend down the canyon attest to the amount of mining done here.

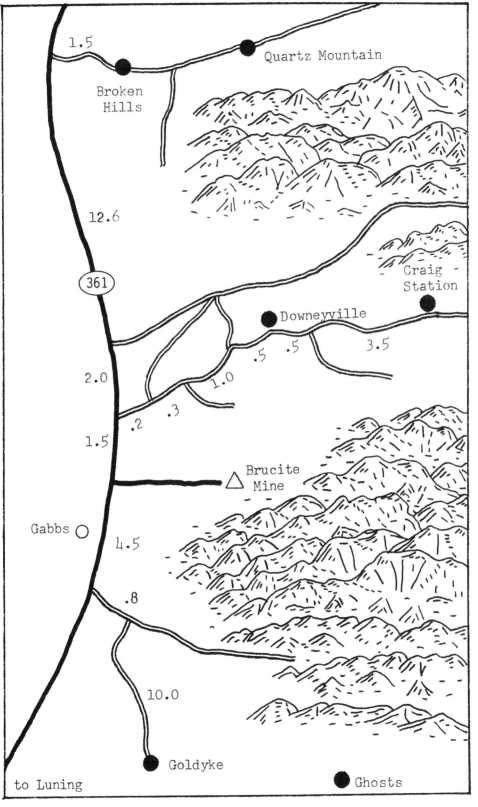

Broken
Hills

1.5

Quartz Mountain

12.6

361

Craig
Station

2.0

Downeyville

.5   .5

3.5

1.0

1.5

.2   .3

Brucite
Mine

Gabbs

4.5

.8

10.0

Goldyke

Ghosts

to Luning

47

BROKEN HILLS - This town was never a rich one, nor was
it a wild town, as so many were.

Gold discoveries were the reason for the town being
built in 1913 and over a span of several years about $75,000
worth of ore was mined.

Several wooden buildings are still standing, all in pretty
fair condition. A little gold can still be mined around here
but hardly enough to make a living in these times of inflation.

RAWHIDE - One of the last big gold strikes in Nevada, Rawhide started to boom in 1907 and in six months had a population of 10,000. Rawhide boasted 90 saloons and Stingaree Gulch at the edge of town boasted 500 chippies.

After one year of existence, a big fire gobbled up about nine square blocks of the business district and many homes. The citizens were undaunted and started rebuilding before the ashes had cooled, and Rawhide bloomed again. But not for long. The gold veins were petering out and the mines closed. Rawhide faded, and out of hundreds of buildings, only a few remain today to remind us of a once great era.

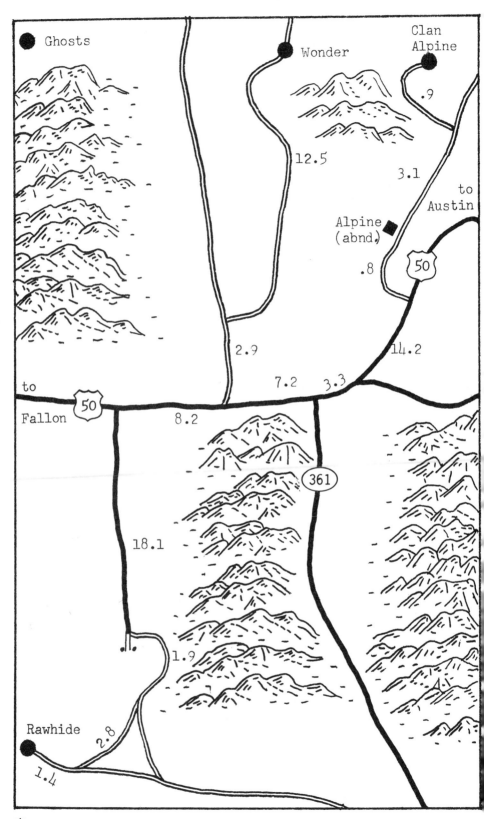

CLAN ALPINE - A town of extremely short duration, born
in 1866 and died in 1867. Rock ruins of the old company office buildings and mill remain and a few house foundations
can be seen.

WONDER - A mining town that came into existence in 1906 and produced $6 million before it faded into oblivion. Most of the buildings were made of wood and have now disappeared from the scene. Trash and rubble extend over a large area here, but the downtown section can be located by the string of dead locust trees that lined the once busy Main Street.

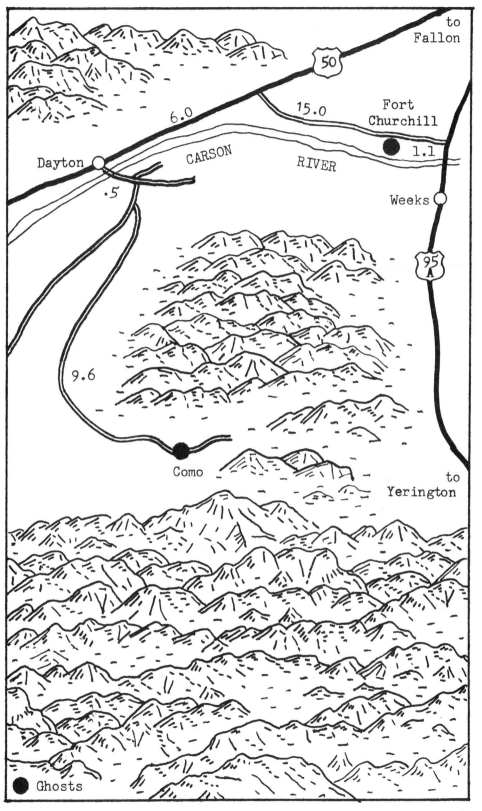

to
Fallon

50

6.0   15.0   Fort
Churchill

Dayton   CARSON   RIVER   1.1

.5   Weeks

95
A

9.6

Como

to
Yerington

Ghosts

53

COMO - A fair sized town that developed in 1863 and boomed to a peak population of 700. By 1874 the town was completely deserted. Como is situated amidst the pine trees in deep snow country. It can be reached by a rough, rocky road, but only in summertime. There are many buildings and ruins scattered over a large area.

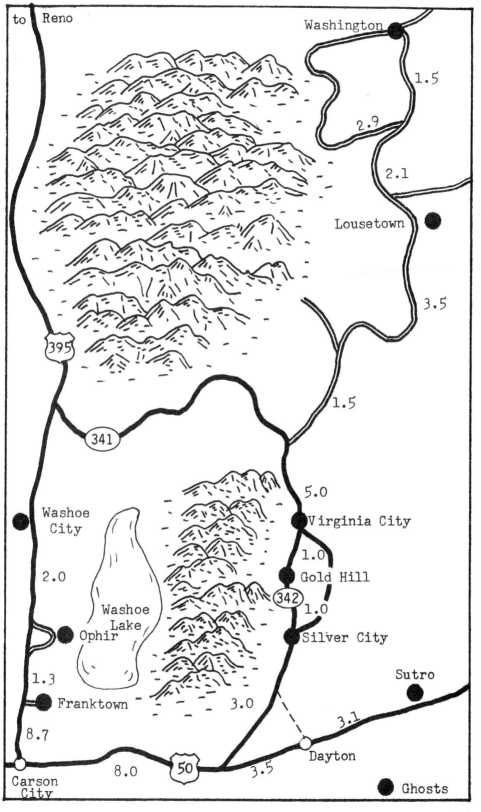

to Reno

Washington

1.5

2.9

2.1

Lousetown

3.5

395

341

1.5

5.0

Washoe City

Virginia City

1.0

Gold Hill

342

2.0

1.0

Washoe Lake

Ophir

Silver City

Sutro

1.3

Franktown

3.0

3.1

8.7

Dayton

50

3.5

Carson City

8.0

Ghosts

55

VIRGINIA CITY - Probably the most commercialized "ghost town" in Nevada, but very interesting and well worth a visit. The town had its beginning in 1859 and the population quickly rose to 3,284 by the time the census was taken in 1861. This is where Nevada's fabulous Comstock Lode was located and the city that was supported by it.

Many famous old buildings are still standing, and the downtown section is much as it was in the 1800's.

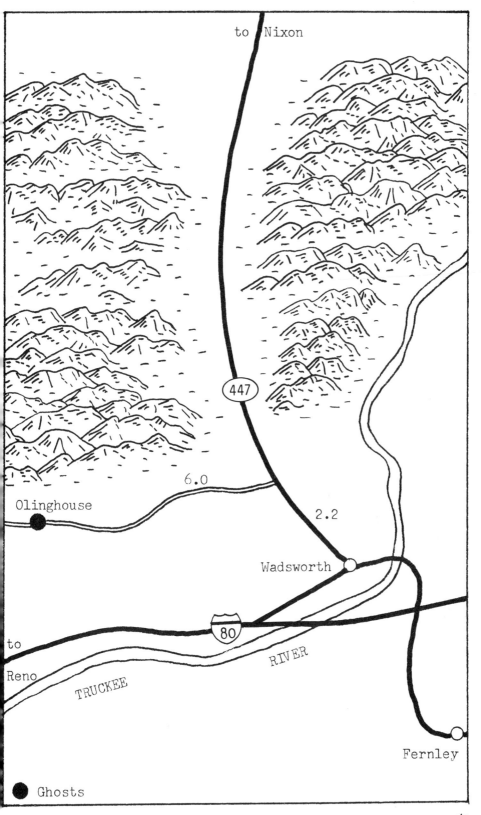

to Nixon

447

Olinghouse

6.0

2.2

Wadsworth

to

Reno

TRUCKEE

RIVER

80

Fernley

● Ghosts

57

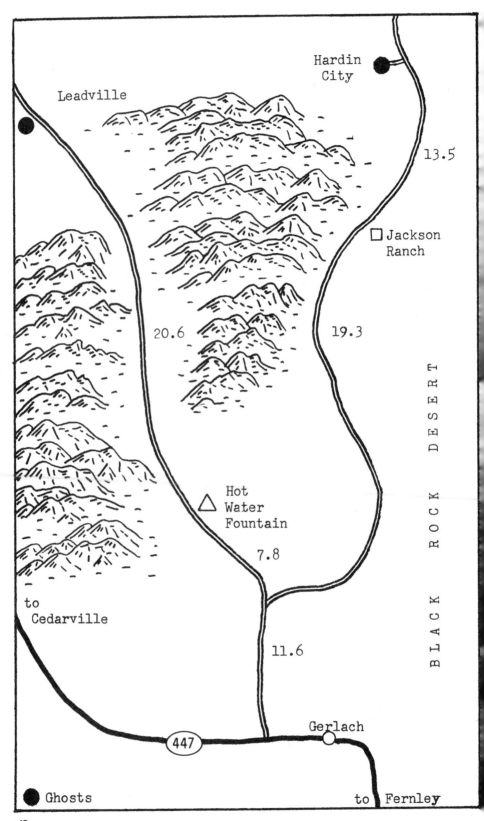

Hardin
City

Leadville

13.5

Jackson
Ranch

20.6

19.3

B
L
A
C
K

R
O
C
K

D
E
S
E
R
T

Hot
Water
Fountain

7.8

to
Cedarville

11.6

Gerlach

447

Ghosts

to Fernley

LEADVILLE - Born in 1909 and abandoned in the 1920's.
The ruins of the old mill can still be seen and several wooden
buildings are still standing, but they are gradually succumb-
ing to the elements.

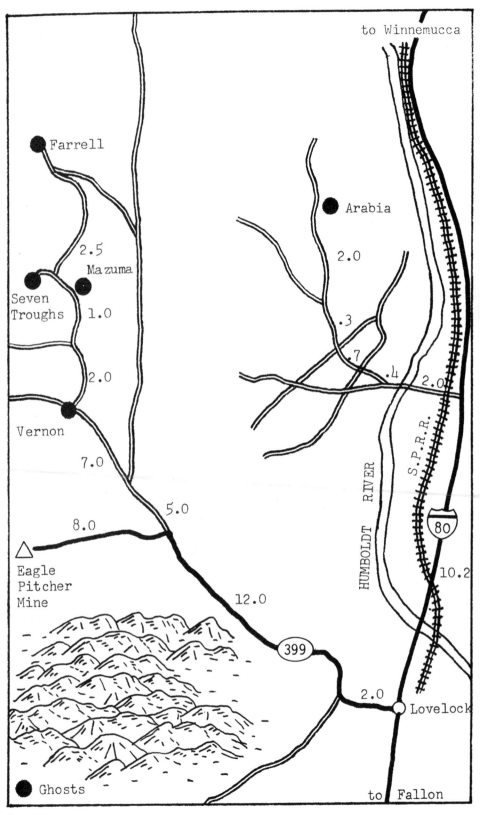

VERNON - The jail and a couple of buildings are left standing at the base of the mountains. Much rubble extends over
a large area. A local rancher told the author in 1966 that the
old jail was still escape proof a year earlier, but some vandals had stolen dynamite from a nearby mine and blew up
the jail.

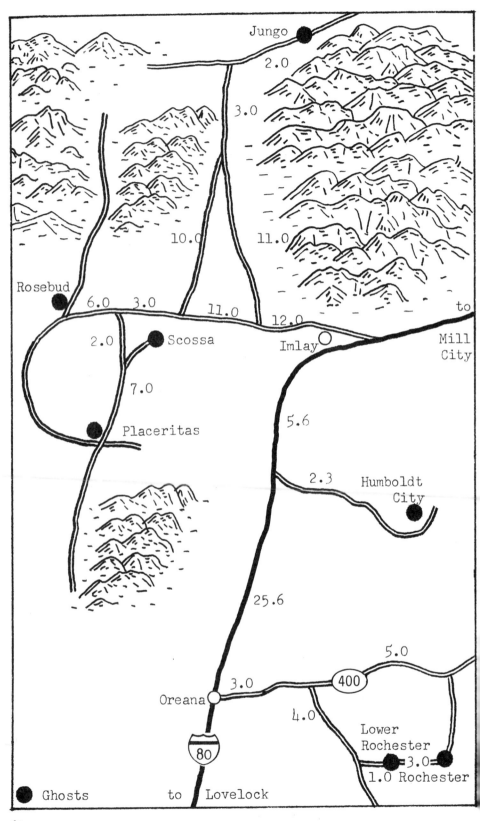

Jungo
2.0
3.0
10.0 11.0
Rosebud 6.0 3.0 11.0 12.0 to
2.0 Scossa Imlay Mill City
7.0
Placeritas 5.6
2.3 Humboldt City
25.6
5.0
400
3.0
Oreana 4.0
80 Lower Rochester
3.0
1.0 Rochester
Ghosts to Lovelock

SCOSSA - Situated in a range of low hills, this town was born
in 1907 when the Scossa brothers discovered gold in the hills.
The old false front drug store still stands, along with a couple
of houses. All are in fair condition.

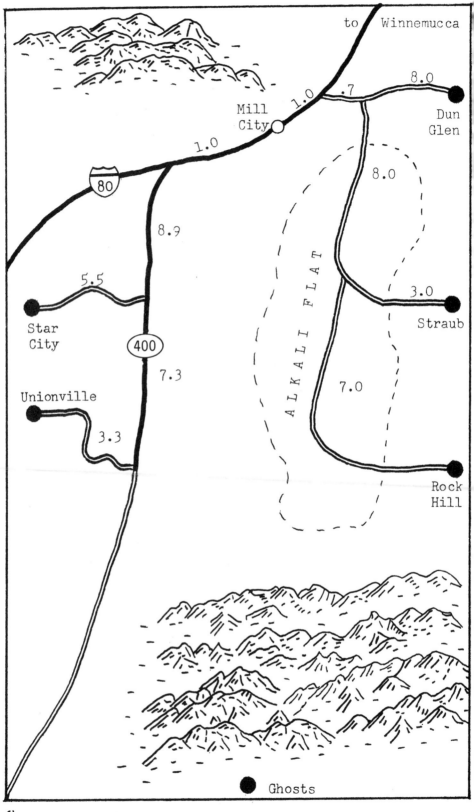

to Winnemucca

Mill City

Dun Glen

8.0

1.0 .7

1.0

8.9

8.0

80

ALKALI FLAT

Star City

5.5

3.0

Straub

400

7.3

Unionville

7.0

3.3

Rock Hill

Ghosts

UNIONVILLE - Nestled in Buena Vista Canyon, this town had its beginning in 1861 when rich silver ores assaying thousands of dollars per ton were discovered in the area. The town boomed to a sizeable population and then faded as most mining towns did.

Only a handful of people are left now. Unionville holds the distinction of having the oldest schoolhouse in Nevada, which has now been turned into a museum. Several of the old buildings, stone walls and many ruins remain.

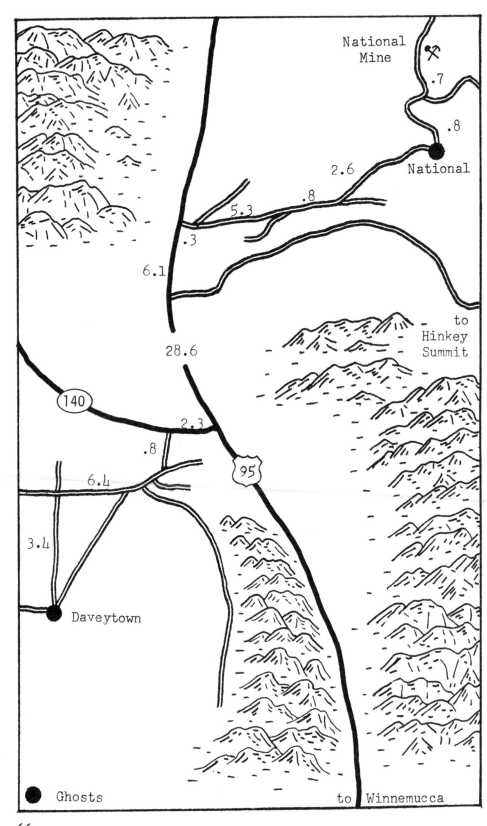

National
Mine

.7

.8

2.6   National

.8

5.3

.3

6.1

to
Hinkey
Summit

28.6

140

2.3

.8

95

6.4

3.4

Daveytown

Ghosts   to Winnemucca

DAVEYTOWN - Gold and silver discoveries in the Slumbering Hills as late as 1925 brought a swarm of prospectors to the area and the town of Daveytown developed. Daveytown is deserted now and only a few wooden buildings are left standing.

NATIONAL - In 1907 an auto-borne prospector drove his National up into the foothills of the Santa Rosa Range about 15 miles south of McDermitt. He discovered gold there and when the word got out, the town of National boomed. The deposits were rich and the mines produced $12 million in gold and silver. The veins finally gave out and so did the town. All that remains today are a few foundations and caved-in cellars.

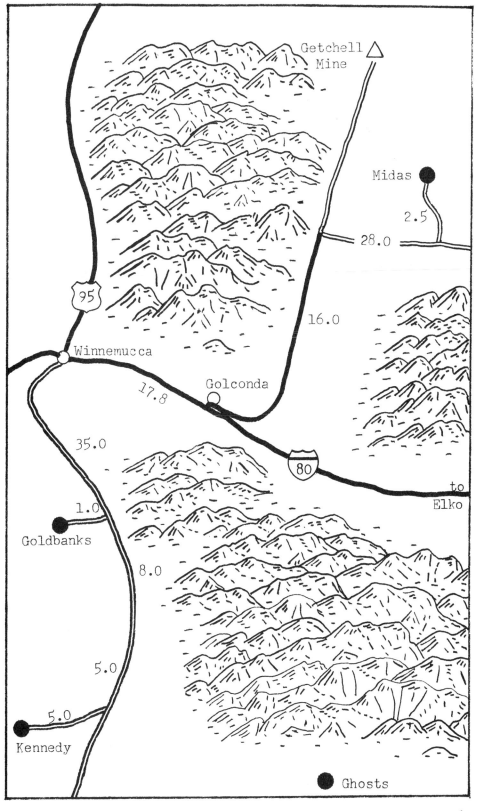

Getchell
Mine

Midas

2.5

28.0

16.0

95

Winnemucca

Golconda

17.8

35.0

80

to
Elko

1.0

Goldbanks

8.0

5.0

5.0

Kennedy

Ghosts

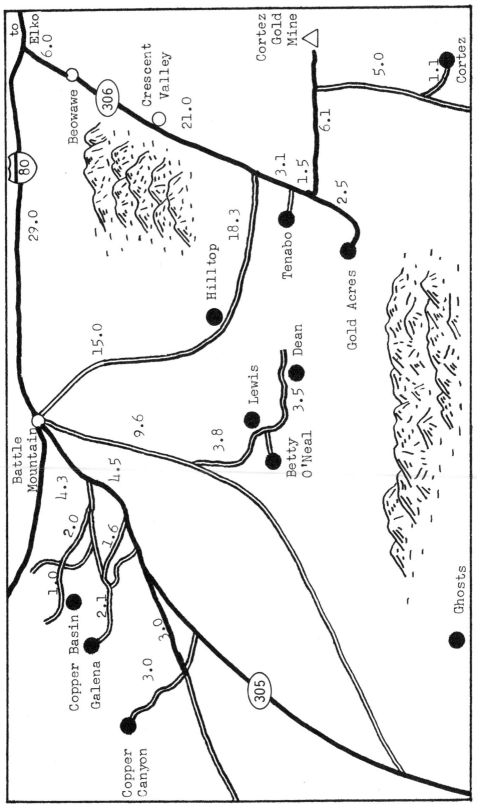

CORTEZ - Immense ore deposits were discovered in 1863 and the town of Cortez developed and soon grew to a population of over 1,000. Cortez was pretty much isolated from the rest of the world and this isolation attracted a lot of rough characters. Killings were frequent and gun play was constant.

The mines operated off and on until 1895 and mining was revived again in 1919. The mines produced over $6 million. A few buildings are left standing today amidst the pinon pines.

71

LEWIS - Gold and silver claims were being worked in 1874
and the town of Lewis developed shortly after. The town
grew to a population of several thousand. The buildings are
gone now and even the foundations are difficult to find.

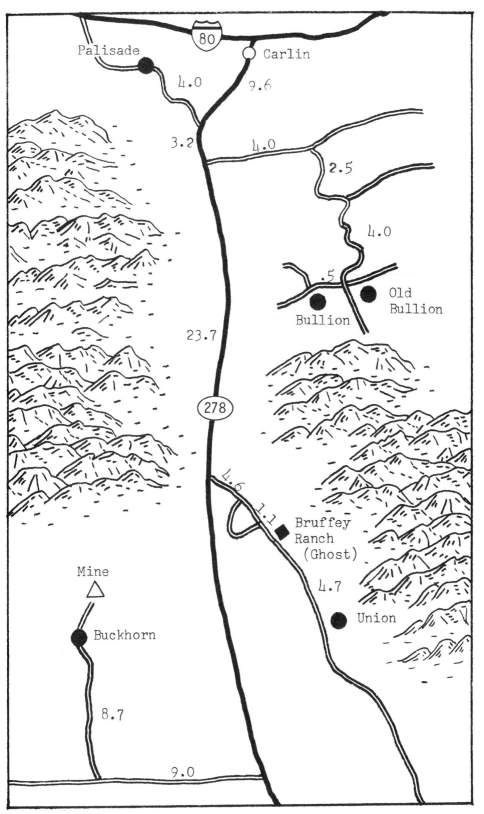

PALISADE - A little railroad town that came into being about 1868 and reached a peak population of 250. This town became an important railhead for supplies to the mining camps and shipments of ores to smelters. Millions of pounds of base metal ingots and much bullion came through Palisade annually.

Several old houses remain, some of them still in pretty good shape.

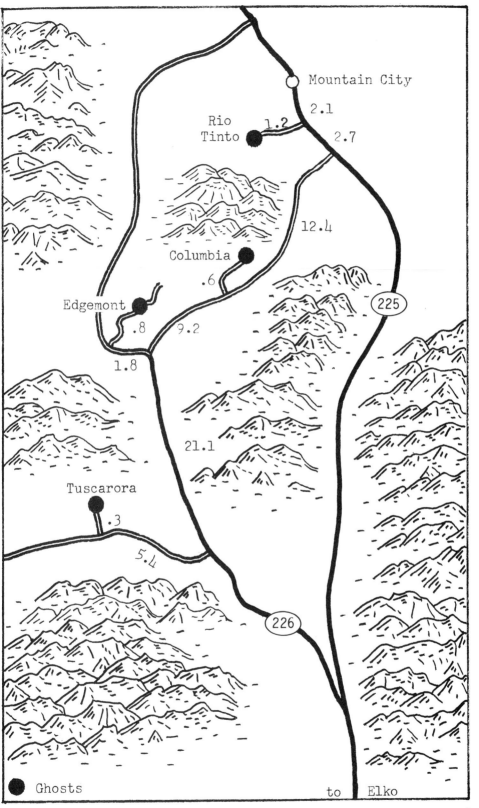

Mountain City

2.1

Rio
Tinto   1.2

2.7

12.4

Columbia

.6

Edgemont

.8   9.2

1.8

225

21.1

Tuscarora

.3

5.4

226

Ghosts   to   Elko

75

TUSCARORA - Rich silver deposits w e r e located on Mt. Blitzen in 1871 and the town of Tuscarora was born. Silver and gold was everywhere and the population soon grew to 5,000. By 1898 Tuscarora had mined $40 million in gold and silver.

Tuscarora had the largest concentration of Chinese in the state of Nevada. The Central Pacific Railroad had imported 10,000 Chinese and when the road was completed, the Chinese were turned loose to shift for themselves. Thousands of them ended up in Tuscarora's Chinatown.

A few people still live in Tuscarora, but she is just a ghost of her former self.

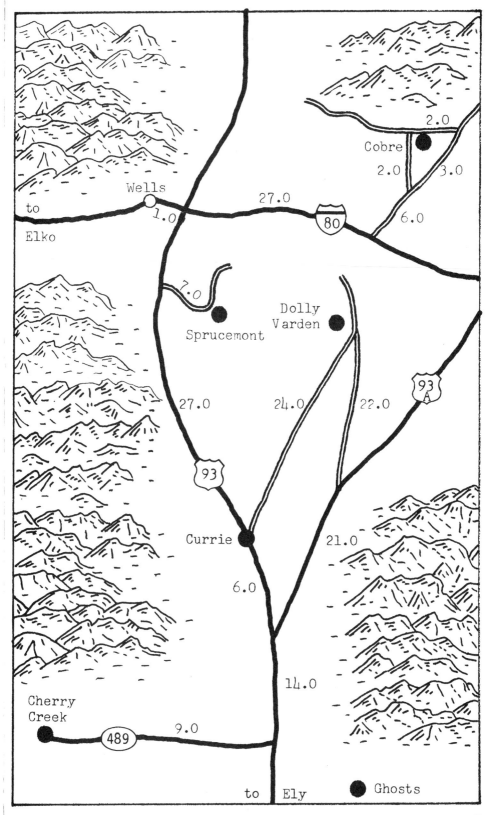

to
Elko

Wells

Cobre

2.0

2.0   3.0

1.0   27.0   **80**   6.0

7.0

Dolly
Varden

Sprucemont

27.0   24.0   22.0   **93 A**

93

Currie   21.0

6.0

14.0

Cherry
Creek

489   9.0

to   Ely   Ghosts

CHERRY CREEK - No c r e e k and certainly no cherries. Where this town got its name is a mystery, but it got its start in 1872 and acquired a population of 6,000. Cherry Creek was a fun town. Lots of girls, booze, horse racing and dancing. People rode as much as 100 miles sometimes to attend the dances and shindigs at Cherry Creek. And when they weren't playing they must have been working, because the records show that the mines gave up about $10 million before the big silver crash which closed the mines and killed the town, along with a lot of other silver mining towns. Several old buildings still stand and a handful of people live here.

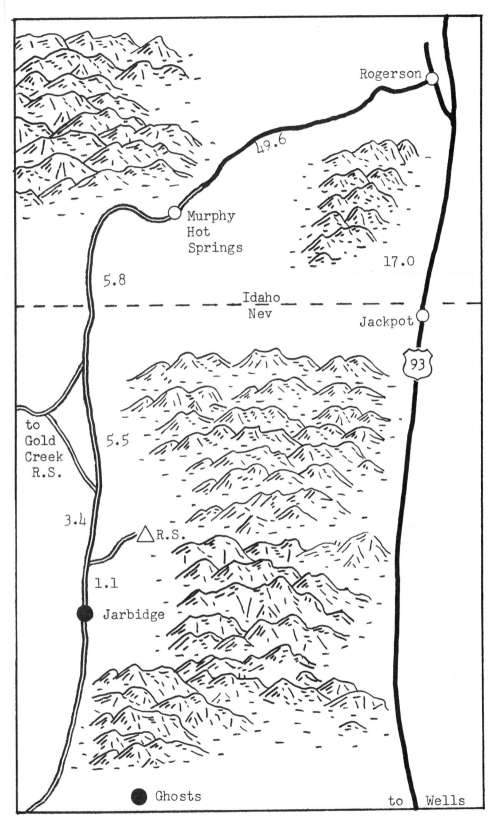

Rogerson

49.6

Murphy
Hot
Springs

17.0

5.8

Idaho
Nev

Jackpot

93

to
Gold
Creek
R.S.

5.5

3.4

△ R.S.

1.1

Jarbidge

Ghosts

to Wells

JARBIDGE - Rich gold veins were discovered in Jarbidge Canyon in 1908 and a rush of prospectors and miners followed, resulting in the formation of the town of Jarbidge. The population grew to over 800 and many millions in gold flowed from the nearby mines.

Jarbidge was plagued by avalanches from the start and the town was nearly wiped out several times from the heavy snows collecting on the slopes of the canyon.

A few people still live in Jarbidge but it is mostly a haven for hunters. The summertime population is small and the wintertime population is smaller.